Selected Songs Wi...

FELIX MENDELSSOHN

Piano Solos by Master Composers of the Period

CONTENTS

Editor: Dale Tucker
Art Design: Joann Carrera
Artwork Reproduced on Cover: *Island in the Sound* by Albert Bierstadt

© 2001 BELWIN-MILLS PUBLISHING CORP. (ASCAP)
All Rights Administered by WARNER BROS. PUBLICATIONS U.S. INC.
All Rights Reserved

Any duplication, adaptation or arrangement of the compositions
contained in this collection requires the written consent of the Publisher.
No part of this book may be photocopied or reproduced in any way without permission.
Unauthorized uses are an infringement of the U.S. Copyright Act and are punishable by law.

FELIX MENDELSSOHN
Born: February 3, 1809 - Hamburg, Germany
Died: November 4, 1847 - Leipzig, Germany

Like many famous composers, Felix Mendelssohn was born into a family with knowledge of music. His mother, Leah, was a pianist, singer, and artist and spoke several languages. His father, Abraham, was a successful banker, and his grandfather was a well-known philosopher. The other three children in the family were also musically talented, each on a different instrument.

When Mendelssohn was only three years old, his family moved to Berlin and converted from Judaism to Christianity. He received piano lessons from his mother while tutors were brought in to teach other instruments and harmony. His father provided the children with strict discipline, and their financial position provided quality education. It was a loving family, and one that often hosted many musicians.

The Mendelssohn home was the scene for many concerts, and the young Felix was often at the piano with small chamber orchestras. Some of his early compositions were performed in this setting. This led to his first public performance at the age of nine, which was met with positive remarks. By twelve Mendelssohn had completed more than fifty compositions including symphonies, sonatas, two operas, a cantata, and others. At fifteen his music tutors said he had outgrown their ability to teach him further. During this time he met the poet Goethe, and a lifelong friendship began.

In 1825, at the age of seventeen, Mendelssohn composed what many consider his masterpiece, the overture to his incidental music to Shakespeare's *A Midsummer Night's Dream.* The "Wedding March" from this is still used today in many weddings around the world. He originally wrote this for two pianos and performed it with his sister, Fanny, but within the year had orchestrated it for a performance he conducted in Stettin. He is also well known for his cantata "Elijah."

Mendelssohn traveled extensively across Europe. These travels and his fond memories of them offered inspiration for many of his orchestral works. Mendelssohn also toured as a conductor, premiering many of his works, including a performance as director of the London Philharmonic Orchestra. In 1836 he was appointed director of the Gewanhaus Orchestra in Leipzig and developed this ensemble into one of the leading orchestras in Europe.

He married the daughter of a minister and they had five children. The family moved to Leipzig after a while, where Mendelssohn organized the Leipzig Conservatory of Music. He also taught piano and composition there yet continued to travel to England, a country he dearly loved, and performed for Queen Victoria.

Mendelssohn lived only thirty-eight years but led a happy and full life. He was considered handsome, well liked, successful in all areas of life, and dedicated to his family. His last years were unfortunately filled with depression and pain, in part from the sudden death of his beloved sister, Fanny. His musical legacy continues strongly today.

SELECTED "SONGS WITHOUT WORDS"

Opus 19, No. 1

FELIX MENDELSSOHN

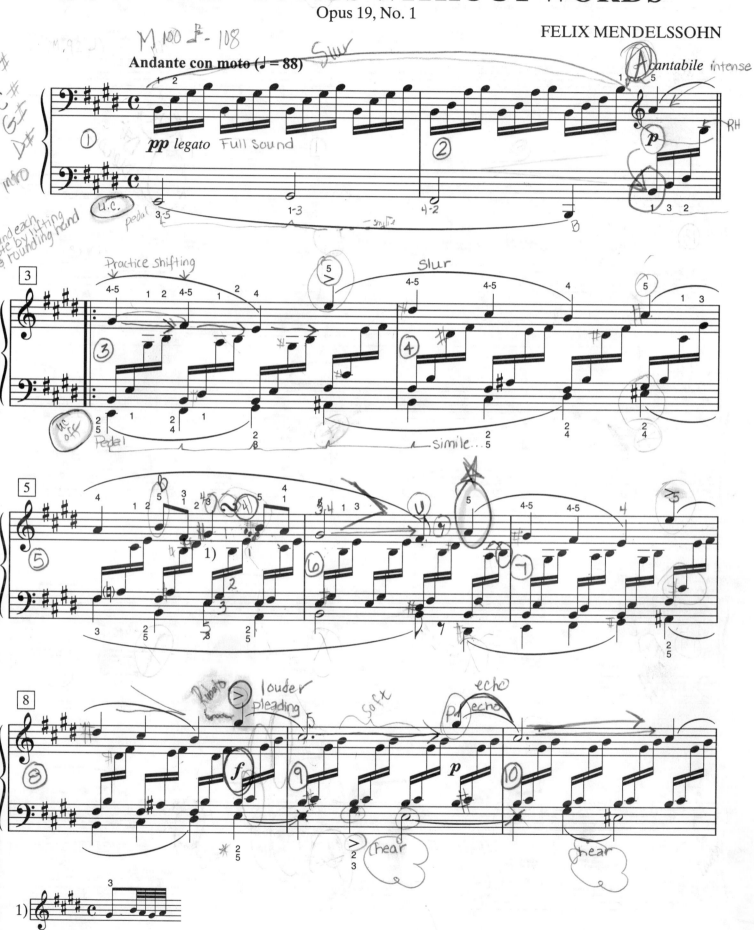

4

ELM01010

VENETIAN BARCAROLE
Opus 19, No. 6

Andante sostenuto (♩. = 96)

SONG WITHOUT WORDS

Opus 30, No. 3

VENETIAN BARCAROLE

Opus 30, No. 6

Allegretto tranquillo (♩. = 69)

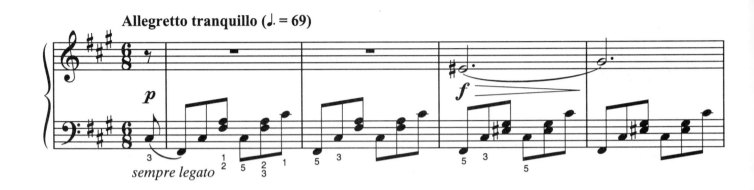

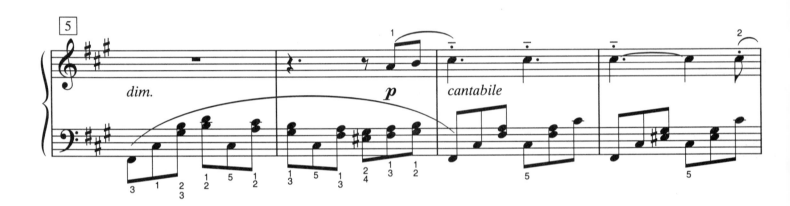

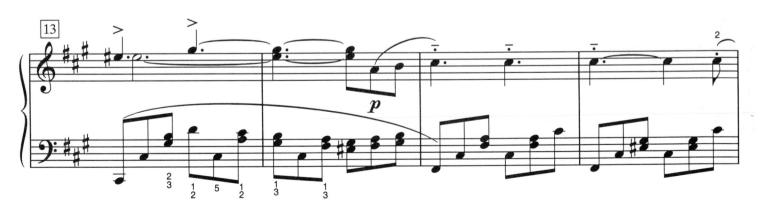

1) The trill begins on the note C♯ in this period.

SONG WITHOUT WORDS

Opus 38, No. 1

16

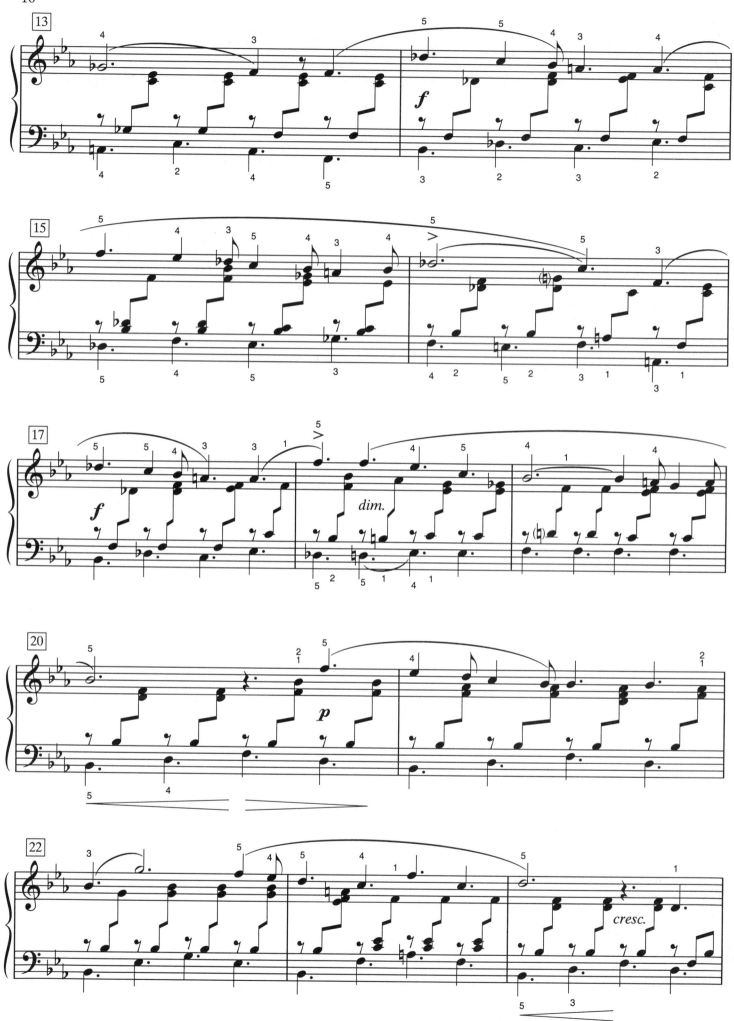

ELM01010

SONG WITHOUT WORDS

Opus 53, No. 3

Presto agitato (♩. = 69)

1) Performed as a grace note in this period, played just before the beat.

POPULAR SONG

Opus 53, No. 5

VENETIAN BARCAROLE

Opus 62, No. 5

SPRING SONG

Opus 62, No. 6

Allegretto grazioso (♩ = 84)

sempre una corda

ELM01010

SONG WITHOUT WORDS
Opus 85, No. 1

1) The pianist has the option of taking various accompanimental notes with the right hand, as edited here, or you may perform the sixteenth-note patterns entirely with the left hand, leaving the right hand free for the melody.

2) Original printings used a single notehead, indicating only one F. Although this represents a 2 against 3 pattern, the final note of the lower voice is not repeated here, and in all similar measures. Mendelssohn intended only a single pitch at the end of these measures.

ELM01010

SONG WITHOUT WORDS

Opus 102, No. 3

1) Performed as a grace note in this period, played just before the beat.

ELM01010

ALBUM-LEAF
Opus 117

1) Performed as grace notes in this period, played just before the beat.

ELM01010

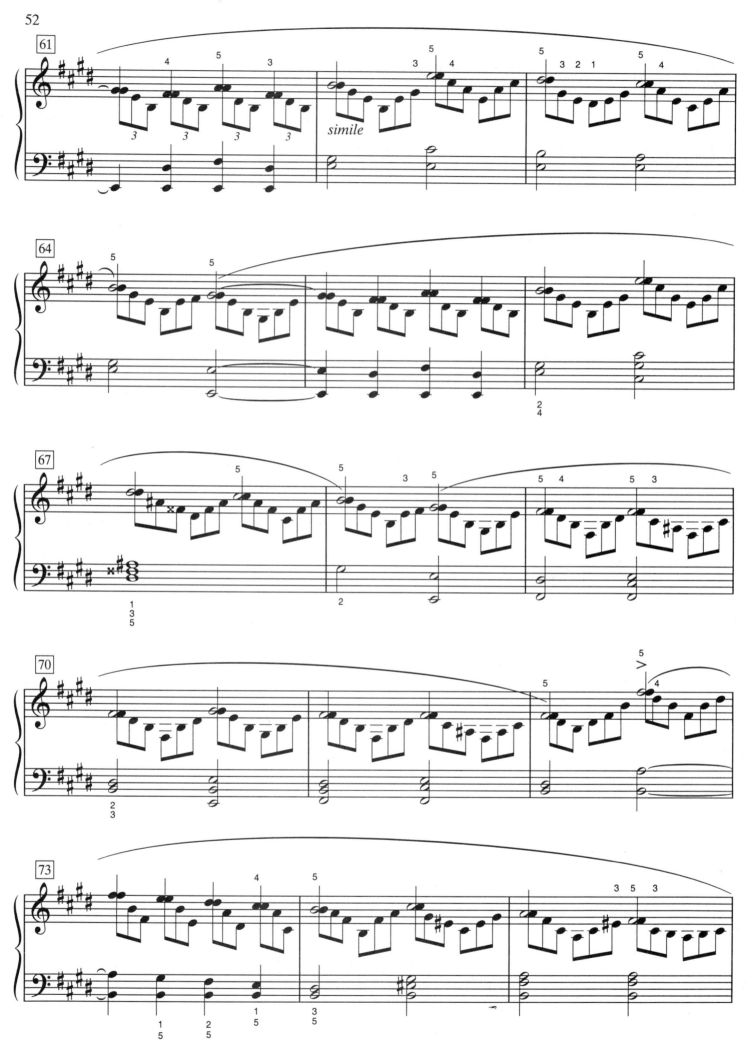

ELM01010